TEACHER'S
Planbook
AND Calendar
of Year-Round Activities

ALICE BERNSTEIN AND
DOROTHY DOUGLAS

Troll

Interior Illustrations by Claude Martinot

This edition published in 2002.

ISBN: 0-8167-3267-1

Printed in the United States of America.

10 9 8 7 6 5 4 3

Contents

Introduction v

Reproducible Calendar Pages

September...6
October 8
November 10
December 12
January 14
February 16
March 18
April..20
May...22
June 24
July 26
August 28

Reproducible Weekly Planner

Weekly Planner Pages 30
Planner Cover 32

Special Days and Activities

September..33
September Events 34
September Activities 35
Where's Fall?..37
My September Newspaper 38

October 39
October Events..40
October Activities 41
Build a Healthy Lunch 43
Whoooo's Inside?...44

November..45
November Events 46
November Activities 47
East Is East and West Is West..48
We Are Thankful 49

December..50
December Events 51
December Activities 52
Bingo! 53
Light a Candle...54

January 55
January Events 56
January Activities 57
I Have a Dream 58
And You Shall Have Some Pie 59

February 60
February Events 61
February Activities 62
Half Hearted Fun 63
Recipe for a Perfect Day 64

March 65
March Events 66
March Activities 67
Happy "I Want You to Be Happy Day" 69

April 70
April Events 71
April Activities 72
My Poem for Earth Day 74
Dots and Dashes 75

May 76
May Events 77
May Activities 78
Flower Power 80
My Mom 81

June 82
June Events 83
June Activities 84
Have a Slice 85
Batty Baseball 86

July 87
July Events 88
July Activities 89
Who's Who? 90
Do Your Part 91

August 92
August Events 93
August Activities 94
Friendship Pop-Up 95
Friendship Pop-Up Pattern 96

Introduction

Planning class activities is easier and more fun when there's something special to celebrate almost every day of the year. This planbook is your guide to both familiar and little-known holidays, anniversaries of interesting events, birthdays of contemporary and historical figures, and many more annual happenings your students will love learning about and celebrating. The book is divided into three sections: **Reproducible Calendar Pages**, the **Reproducible Weekly Planner**, and the **Special Days and Activities** section with a wide variety of suggested activities and reproducibles to help you make every day a special event.

Here's how to use your **Teacher's Planbook and Calendar of Year-Round Activities**.

1. Find this month in the **Reproducible Calendar Pages** section. On the perforations, tear out the two calendar pages for the month. Make a copy of each page, and tape your copied pages together.

2. Write the dates for this month in the small squares on the calendar grid.

3. Turn to the first page for this month in the **Special Days and Activities** section to find a famous quote to share with your class this month.

4. Decide which special days and events you'd like to celebrate with your class, and write them on your calendar. Use the calendar to keep track of your own special days, too—appointments, meetings, parent conferences, students' birthdays, class trips, etc.

5. Each week, duplicate the **Weekly Planner Pages**. Fill in the dates, and use these professional pages to outline your lesson plans. The **Planner Cover** makes an attractive cover or title page for your lesson plans. Punch holes in the planner pages and planner cover. Use paper fasteners to hold them together, or keep them in a three-ring binder.

6. Use the activity pages and reproducibles to make every month special for your students.

SEPTEMBER

Monday	Tuesday	Wednesday

Thursday	Friday	Sat	Sun

OCTOBER

Monday	Tuesday	Wednesday

Thursday	Friday	Sat	Sun

  # NOVEMBER

Monday	Tuesday	Wednesday

Thursday	Friday	Sat	Sun

DECEMBER

Monday	Tuesday	Wednesday

Thursday	Friday	Sat	Sun

JANUARY

Monday	Tuesday	Wednesday

Thursday	Friday	Sat	Sun

FEBRUARY

Monday	Tuesday	Wednesday

Thursday	Friday	Sat	Sun

MARCH

Monday	Tuesday	Wednesday

Thursday	Friday	Sat	Sun

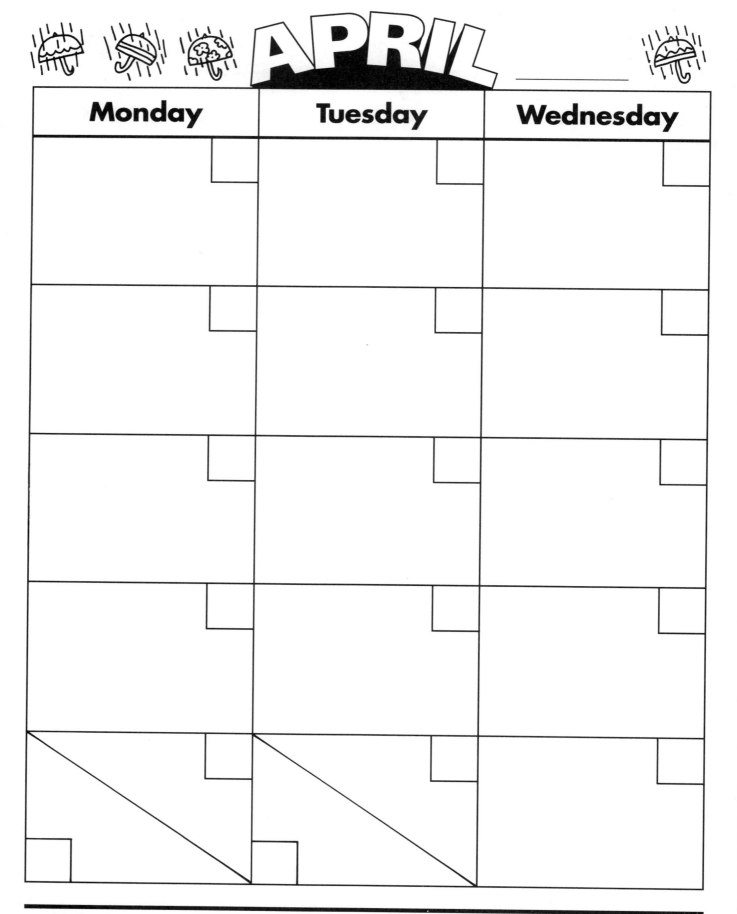

APRIL

Monday	Tuesday	Wednesday

Thursday	Friday	Sat	Sun

MAY

Monday	Tuesday	Wednesday

Thursday	Friday	Sat	Sun

  # JUNE

Monday	Tuesday	Wednesday

Thursday	Friday	Sat	Sun

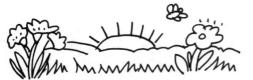 

JULY _____

Monday	Tuesday	Wednesday

Thursday	Friday	Sat	Sun

AUGUST

Monday	Tuesday	Wednesday

Thursday	Friday	Sat	Sun

Name _____ **Week of** _____

	Subject:		
Monday			
Tuesday			
Wednesday			
Thursday			
Friday			

Subject:		

Lesson Plans

Teacher _____

Class _____

Asters, deep purple,
A grasshopper's call,
Today it is summer,
Tomorrow is fall.

—from "September,"
by Edwina Fallis

September Is . . .

Library Card Sign-up Month
All-American Breakfast Month
Ice Cream Month

National Courtesy Month
Women of Achievement Month
National Hispanic Heritage Month

Special Weeks in September

Constitution Week (week beginning September 17)
National Mind Mapping and Brainstorming Week (third full week)

Special Days in September

Labor Day America's workers are saluted the first Monday of the month.

National Grandparents Day Grandparents are recognized on the first Sunday after Labor Day.

Native American Day The United States's first residents are honored on the fourth Friday of the month.

National Good Neighbor Day Neighborliness is promoted on the fourth Sunday of September.

Rosh Hashanah The beginning of the Jewish New Year falls in September or October.

Yom Kippur Jewish Day of Atonement falls ten days after Rosh Hashanah.

First day of autumn falls on September 22 or 23.

September Events

1   **The last carrier pigeon** died at the Cincinnati Zoo in 1914.

3   **Aliki**, children's author and illustrator, was born in 1920.

4   **Newspaper Carrier Day** honors those who deliver our newspapers.

5   **Be Late for Something Day**, sponsored by the Procrastination Club of America, encourages everyone to slow down and enjoy life.

6   **Jane Addams**, the American social worker who organized settlement houses for the poor in Chicago, was born in 1860.

7   **Grandma Moses**, American primitive painter, was born in 1860.

8   **National Pledge of Allegiance Day** commemorates the publication of the pledge, in 1892, in *Youth's Companion* magazine.

9   **California Admission Day** (31st state, 1850).

10   **Swap Ideas Day** is set aside to encourage people to share creative ideas that will benefit humanity.

11   **No News Is Good News Day**, sponsored by the Wellness Permission League, is a day to skip the bad news on television or in newspapers.

13   **Roald Dahl**, the British author of such favorite children's books as *Matilda* and *Charlie and the Chocolate Factory*, was born in 1916.

15   Two children's authors were born on this day. **Robert McCloskey**, author of *Make Way for Ducklings* and *Blueberries for Sal*, was born in 1914. • Born in 1934, **Tomie dePaola** wrote and illustrated such popular children's books as *Strega Nona* and *Pancakes for Breakfast*.

16   **The Mayflower** left Plymouth, England for the New World in 1620.

17   **Constitution Week** begins today to commemorate the signing of the Constitution in 1787. • **Citizenship Day** celebrates the rights and duties described in the Constitution.

21   Celebrate **World Gratitude Day**, which encourages a spirit of gratitude around the world.

22   In 1789, the United States established the **first U.S. Post Office** in New York City. • In 1903, Italo Marchiony, in New York City, invented the **first ice cream cone**.

24   The **U.S. Supreme Court** was established in 1789.

25   The **first newspaper in America** was published in 1690. • In 1981, **Sandra Day O'Connor**, the first woman on the Supreme Court, was sworn in.

26   **Johnny Appleseed**, planter of orchards, was born in 1774. • **National Good Neighbor Day** encourages a friendly spirit to the folks nearby.

27   Patriot of the American Revolution, **Samuel Adams**, was born in 1722. • **Ancestor Appreciation Day** is set aside for people to learn more about their ancestors.

30   **Babe Ruth hit his 60th home run** of the season on this day in 1927, a record that wasn't beaten until 1961.

September Activities

Library Card Sign-up Month Plan a class trip to the local library this month. Ask the children to bring in their library cards so that you can identify those who still need one. Help these children fill out the forms they need to get a card and check out books.

All-American Breakfast Month Help the children plan a delicious and wholesome breakfast for the class.

National Courtesy Month and **National Mind Mapping and Brainstorming Week** Use brainstorming and mind mapping techniques to help the class create a poster or bulletin board of common courtesies that will help the class run smoothly for the rest of the year. Explain that brainstorming and mind mapping are ways for everyone to contribute many ideas about a subject without interruption or criticism—a wonderful and workable courtesy. On the chalkboard, begin several mind maps for the class: classroom courtesies, hallway courtesies, cafeteria courtesies, playground courtesies. Then have students fill in their ideas in circles on the mind map. Vote on the best ideas to include on a series of posters for National Courtesy Month.

During **National Hispanic Heritage Month** display a map that includes Mexico, Puerto Rico, Central and South America. Ask Hispanic members of your class to affix colored stick-on dots to places from which their families came or still live.

Labor Day is celebrated with a day off from work this month. Soon after this holiday, ask the children to write or tell what this school day would be like if no one worked at all.

National Grandparents Day Ask the children to remember their grandparents or older relatives and neighbors by designing a greeting card in honor of this day.

Native American Day, the fourth Friday of the month, is a good day to teach the class words that come from Native American languages: *opossum, toboggan, pecan, raccoon, moose, chipmunk, squash, skunk.*

September 3 Celebrate the birthday of **Aliki**, the children's book author and illustrator, by reading aloud one of her books. Some good ones for this time of year: *Corn is Maize, The Many Lives of Ben Franklin, The Story of Johnny Appleseed.*

September 8 National Pledge of Allegiance Day Pledge allegiance to the American flag on this day. Then write the Pledge on the chalkboard and ask the children to discuss what they think the words mean.

Constitution Week, Sept. 17-23, and **Citizenship Day, Sept. 17**, provide the opportunity for children to learn about the Constitution and the responsibilities of citizenship—voting, obeying laws, paying taxes. Have the children contribute ideas and work on a hallway poster called "Being a Good School Citizen."

September 22 or 23 The **first day of autumn** is the perfect time for a walk outdoors to look for signs that fall is here. Use **reproducible** activity page 37 as a checklist for finding fall's first signs. Wind up your fall outing by reading Chris Van Allsburg's *The Stranger*, a haunting story about a year when fall doesn't arrive on time.

September 25 The **first newspaper in America** was published on this day. Have each student write a front page about his or her experiences at school this month. See **reproducible** activity page 38.

September 26 Tell children that today you want to celebrate the birthday of John Chapman, as well as **Good Neighbor Day**. Explain that Chapman was also known as **Johnny Appleseed** because he travelled through the Midwest planting orchards and handing out seeds to people he met. In honor of his birthday, tell the class you will bring in enough apples to cut into quarters for your class and the class next door. Have the students figure out how many apples you will need for both classes. Read Aliki's *Johnny Appleseed* while your class and your "good neighbors" enjoy their apples.

Name _____   Date _____

Where's Fall?

Can you find fall? Go for a walk. Look for signs of fall. Color and check off the ones you find. Add your own pictures of fall to this page.

☐ **Monarch butterflies**

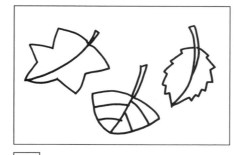

☐ **Falling leaves**

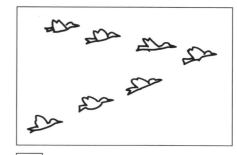

☐ **Flocks of birds**

☐ **Leaves changing color**

☐ **Pumpkins**

☐ **Halloween decorations**

Do you see other signs of fall? Write or draw them here:

Name _____   Date _____

My September Newspaper

MY SCHOOL FRIENDS

MY STORY

FUN I HAD AT SCHOOL

BOOKS I READ

OCTOBER

October gave a party;
The leaves by hundreds came;
The ashes, oaks, and maples,
And those of every name.

—*from "October's Party,"
by George Cooper*

October Is . . .

Computer Learning Month
Energy Awareness Month
National Pizza Month

Consumer Information Month
National Stamp Month

Special Weeks in October

Get Organized Week (first full week)
Fire Prevention Week (first full week)
National Metric Week (second full week)
National School Lunch Week (second full week)
National Pet Peeve Week (second full week)
International Letter-Writing Week (second full week)
Peace, Friendship, and Good Will Week (last week)

Special Days in October

Universal Children's Day A day designated on the first Monday of October to promote "worldwide fraternity and understanding among children."

Child Health Day A day set aside on the first Monday of October to promote the good health of children.

October Events

1 The **first post card** was issued by the Austrian post office in 1869. • In 1924, **Jimmy Carter**, the nation's 39th president, was born.

2 **Mohandas Gandhi**, the Indian spiritual and political leader honored worldwide for his promotion of nonviolent resistance, was born in 1869. • **Name Your Car Day** is set aside for everyone to honor the family car by giving it a pet name.

4 **Edward Stratemeyer**, the creator of The Hardy Boys and Nancy Drew, was born in 1862.

5 Children's authors born today are **Robert Lawson**, author of Newbery Medal winner, *Rabbit Hill*, born in 1892, and **Donald Sobol**, born in 1924, and creator and author of the Encyclopedia Brown series.

6 Happy birthday to American inventor, **George Westinghouse**, born in 1846.

10 Children's book illustrator, **James Marshall**, was born in 1942 and went on to illustrate such favorite series as the Miss Nelson books, the George and Martha books, and the Stupids books.

11 Activist and humanitarian, **Eleanor Roosevelt**, was born in 1884. • Canadians, who celebrate their harvest a month earlier than Americans, give thanks for their bounty on **Thanksgiving Day**.

12 Italian explorer, **Christopher Columbus,** sailing under the Spanish flag, landed on what is now San Salvador Island in the Bahamas.

13 **Molly Pitcher** (Mary Ludwig Hays), who tended the American rebels in the battlefield with medicine, food, and water during the Revolutionary War, was born in 1754.

14 Supreme Commander of Allied Forces in World War II and the 34th president of the United States, **Dwight D. Eisenhower**, was born in 1890. • On this day in 1893, children's author of The Littles series, **Lois Lenski**, was born.

15 Happy birthday to **Winnie the Pooh**, who first appeared in print in 1926. • That's enough to cheer up any grouch, especially on **National Grouch Day**, which generously recognizes those grumpy folks.

16 **Dictionary Day** commemorates the birthday, in 1758, of **Noah Webster**, the American teacher, journalist, and lexicographer who compiled the *Webster's Dictionary*.

19 The Wellness Permission League founded **Evaluate Your Life Day** to encourage people to see if their lives are going in the right direction.

21 **Thomas Edison** brightened the world when he lit an **incandescent lamp** for thirteen and a half hours in 1879.

27 The 26th president of the United States, **Theodore Roosevelt,** was born in 1858.

30 Founding Father, **John Adams**, the second president of the United States, and father of John Quincy Adams, the sixth U.S. president, was born in 1735 and died on the same day as Thomas Jefferson, July 4, 1826.

31 All Hallow's Eve, better known as **Halloween**, is an ancient autumn celebration that takes place on this day. • **Nevada Admission Day** (36th state, 1864).

October Activities

National School Lunch Month Hand out copies of the Food Pyramid. (See **reproducible** activity page 43.) Ask students what they ate for lunch in the last few days that might fit into a pyramid. Over the next month, ask the children to draw or glue onto the pyramid magazine pictures of healthy lunch foods they eat. At the end of the month, plan a Healthful Lunch Day where the class shares healthful items from each food group.

Get Organized Week Set aside ten minutes a day for students to reorganize just one thing each day: a locker, a desk, a notebook, or a small area of the classroom.

National Metric Week Post a banner on the bulletin board that says: ONE FOOT = HOW MANY CENTIMETERS? In Canada go from metric to imperial measurements: ONE HUNDRED CENTIMETERS = HOW MANY INCHES? Then have each student trace the outline of one foot onto paper or posterboard, then measure it, and write down the measurement in the middle of the cutout. Display the footprints under the bulletin-board banner.

Universal Children's Day On this day, tell the class you are taking a survey of what children have in common. Arrange the class into pairs. Give the pairs ten minutes to brainstorm and list things they have in common—everything from the same middle initial, for example, to a birthday in the same month or a parent with curly hair. Then have the pairs share their lists. Encourage students to discuss what they might have in common with children in other parts of the world.

October 5 Wish Encyclopedia Brown creator, **Donald Sobol**, a happy birthday by reading aloud a mystery from his series. As you read, have the children list clues on the chalkboard. Before you get to the end, see if the class can guess the solution.

October 10 Celebrate the life of **James Marshall**, the children's book illustrator, by having an unannounced "Miss Nelson Day." Come to class in a silly outfit. Read *Miss Nelson is Missing!* or *Miss Nelson is Back* before you slip out to change from your "substitute teacher" disguise into your regular clothes.

October 16 Remember **Noah Webster** on **Dictionary Day** by playing a dictionary game, "Animal, Vegetable, or Mineral." Organize students into small groups with one dictionary per group. Write these words on the chalkboard: adder, agate, basalt, kelp, linden, moray, obsidian, sloth, steed, tern, yucca, zebu. Hand each group a sheet of paper with this heading across the top: ANIMAL VEGETABLE MINERAL. Have students take turns finding a word in the dictionary, reading aloud the definition, and writing the definition under the appropriate heading. For younger students, organize the game as a scavenger hunt by giving the page number where the word appears and reading the definition out loud when a group finds a word. Invite the group that first found the word to guess the category in which the word belongs.

October 19 Announce that today is **Evaluate Your Life Day** as you hand out blank sheets of paper. Ask your students to draw an arrow across the sheet that says "Right Way" and another arrow pointing in the opposite direction that says "Wrong Way." Tell students to list what they are doing right in life on the "Right Way" arrow and things they would like to fix in their lives on the "Wrong Way" arrow. Tell them to check their sheets from time to time to see if they're going in the direction they want.

October 27 Celebrate **Theodore Roosevelt's birthday**. Invite the children to bring teddy bears to class on this day. Explain that a toy maker created the first teddy bear ever for Theodore Roosevelt, after the toy maker read that Roosevelt, a rugged outdoorsman and hunter, refused to shoot a bear cub during a hunting trip.

October 31 Booooo! It's **Halloween**. Hand out **reproducible** activity page 44. Ask the children to draw some of the Halloween characters they expect to see in the windows of the haunted house.

Name _____   Date _____

Build a Healthy Lunch

Eat foods that are good for you. Choose things from this food pyramid every day.
You can eat a lot from the bottom of the pyramid and smaller amounts from the top.
Look in magazines for pictures of foods that belong in each section. Paste or draw
the foods that belong in each part.

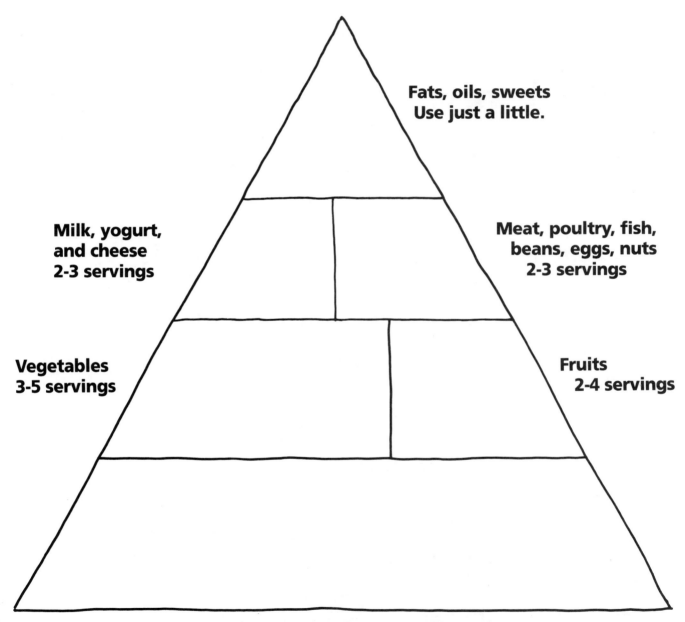

**Fats, oils, sweets
Use just a little.**

**Milk, yogurt,
and cheese
2-3 servings**

**Meat, poultry, fish,
beans, eggs, nuts
2-3 servings**

**Vegetables
3-5 servings**

**Fruits
2-4 servings**

Bread, cereal, rice, and pasta 6-10 servings

Name _____   Date _____

Whoooo's Inside?

Change this house into a haunted house. Cut the windows along the dotted lines.
Tape a piece of plain paper underneath each window. Open the window. Draw
some Halloween characters inside.

November woods are bare and still;
November days are clear and bright;
Each noon burns up the morning's chill,
The morning's snow is gone by night.

—*from "November Woods,"*
by Helen Hunt Jackson

November Is . . .

Aviation History Month	Doll Collection Month
Good Nutrition Month	Child Safety and Protection Month
International Creative Child and Adult Month	

Special Weeks in November

Cat Week (first full week)
National Chemistry Week (second full week)
National Geography Awareness Week (third full week)
National Children's Book Week (third full week)
American Education Week (third full week)

Special Days in November

Election Day (first Tuesday)
Thanksgiving Day, United States (fourth Thursday)

November Events

1 **National Authors' Day** celebrates the contributions of writers to our literary heritage. • The **U.S. Weather Bureau** made the first weather observation in 1870.

2 **North Dakota Admission Day** (39th state, 1889) and **South Dakota Admission Day** (40th state, 1889).

3 **Sandwich Day** honors the fourth Earl of Sandwich, inventor of the sandwich, born in 1718.

4 Englishman, Howard Carter, discovered **King Tut's Tomb** in Luxor, Egypt in 1922.

6 **Saxophone Day** celebrates the birthday of **Adolphe Sax**, a Belgian musician and musical instrument inventor, born in 1814. • American composer and band leader, **John Philip Sousa**, who composed the patriotic marches, "Semper Fidelis," and "Stars and Stripes Forever," was born on this day in 1854.

7 Polish scientist, **Marie Curie**, the first person to win two Nobel Prizes, was born in 1867.

8 A pun day to play with words is **Abet and Aid Punsters Day**, sponsored by Punsters Unlimited. • **X Rays** were discovered by German physicist, Wilhelm Roentgen, in 1895. • **Montana Admission Day** (41st state, 1889).

9 The **Berlin Wall**, separating East and West Berlin in Germany, was opened in 1989.

10 Children's educational program, **"Sesame Street"** first aired in 1969.

11 **Veterans Day** in the United States and **Remembrance Day** in Canada both commemorate their countries' war veterans • **Abigail Smith Adams**, wife of John Adams, second president of the United States and

mother of John Quincy Adams, sixth president of the United States, was born in 1744. • **Washington Admission Day**, (42nd state, 1889).

12 **Auguste Rodin**, French sculptor, was born in Paris, France in 1840.

13 Author of *Treasure Island*, **Robert Louis Stevenson**, was born in Scotland in 1850.

14 French Impressionist painter, **Claude Monet**, was born in 1840.

15 **Georgia O'Keeffe**, American painter who was inspired by the great beauty of the American desert landscape, was born in 1887.

16 **National Community Education Day** promotes relationships between schools and their communities. • **Oklahoma Admission Day** (46th state, 1907).

17 **National Educational Support Personnel Day** recognizes the contributions of school-support employees.

21 **World Hello Day** promotes personal communication by encouraging every person to say hello to at least 10 other people. • **North Carolina Ratification Day** (12th state, 1789).

22 The nation mourned when President **John F. Kennedy** was slain in Dallas, Texas in 1963.

26 Evangelist and former slave, **Sojourner Truth**, who spent her life promoting women's rights and fighting for the abolition of slavery, died in 1883 in Battle Creek, Michigan.

29 Author of *Little Women*, **Louisa May Alcott**, was born in Pennsylvania in 1832.

30 **Winston Churchill,** British statesman, Prime Minister during World War II, was born in Oxfordshire, England in 1874.

November Activities

Recognize Child Safety and Protection Month by having your students brainstorm ideas for playground safety rules. Ask the class to create posters to display in the playground.

Cat Week Ask the class to think of cat sayings that have crept into our language "on little cat feet." To "let the cat out of the bag" start the list with some of these: "copycats," "raining cats and dogs," "playing cat and mouse," "cat got your tongue." Ask the cat lovers in your class to explain what these sayings mean.

National Geography Awareness Week Write "North," "South," "East," and "West" on separate sheets of paper. Tape them to the appropriate walls or windows in the classroom. Have students take turns standing in the middle of the room to describe an item that is north, south, east, or west of him or her. At the end of the game, hand out copies of **reproducible** activity page 48 for the students to complete. Answer: GLOBE

Thanksgiving Day, United States Set aside time for the children to think about what they are thankful for. Give them copies of **reproducible** activity page 49 to express their thanks.

November 3 Sandwich Day To celebrate the fourth Earl of Sandwich's birthday, have sandwiches for a snack. Ask each student to bring in a favorite sandwich he or she created.

November 6 To the taped accompaniment of some **John Philip Sousa** marches, march around the schoolyard to celebrate his birthday. Make it a double birthday celebration by inviting any saxophone-playing students to play a note or two in honor of **Adolphe Sax**.

November 12 Auguste Rodin's Birthday Show the class a picture of Rodin's famous statue, "The Thinker." Ask for volunteers to pose as these fanciful statues: "The Writer," "The Singer," "The Runner," "The Dancer."

November 13 To teach map skills for **National Geography Awareness Week** *and* celebrate the birth of *Treasure Island* author, **Robert Louis Stevenson**, hide a treasure that the class can share—bags of raisins, colorful art supplies. Hand out directional clues that lead to the treasure.

November 17 National Young Reader's Day Ask each student to create a poster with the title of one favorite book that he or she has read and a one-sentence recommendation. Display the poster near your classroom bookshelves.

Name _____   Date _____

East Is East And West Is West

Can you find NORTH, SOUTH, EAST, and WEST directions on a map? Practice reading directions by playing this game. Put your pencil in the center square to start the game. Then follow the steps.

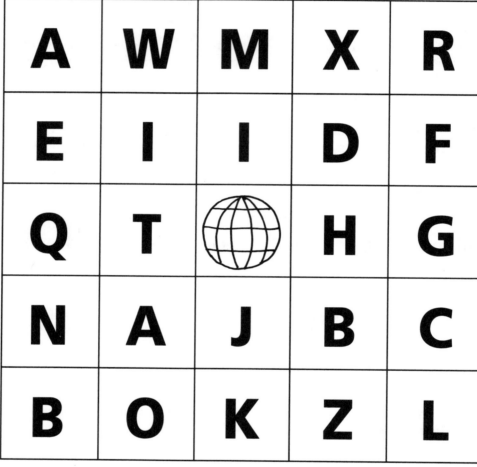

1. Go two blocks EAST and circle the letter.
2. Got two blocks SOUTH and circle the letter.
3. Got three blocks WEST and circle the letter.
4. Go one block WEST and circle the letter.
5. Go three blocks NORTH and circle the letter.

Write the circled letters in the blanks. What word do they spell? _____ _____ _____ _____ _____

Name _____   Date _____

We Are Thankful

Can you think of three things to be thankful for on Thanksgiving Day? Write them in the spaces. Then draw pictures.

I am thankful for _____ .

I am thankful for _____ .

I am thankful for _____ .

DECEMBER

The willows hanging low,
Shake from their long and trailing skirts
The freshly fallen snow.

—from "Willows in the Snow,"
by Tsuru

December is . . .
Bingo Month

Special Weeks in December
Human Rights Week (end of the first, beginning of the second week)
Tell Someone They're Doing a Good Job Week (second full week)

Special Days in December
Hanukkah This eight-day Jewish celebration is called the Festival of Lights.
The first day of winter falls on December 21 or 22.

December Events

1 The **first skywriting** appeared in 1922. • **Rosa Parks**, a black woman, refused to give up her bus seat to a white man in Montgomery, Alabama in 1955. Her arrest led to a boycott that launched the civil rights movement.

2 French painter, **Georges Seurat**, who abandoned the Impressionist style to develop the pointillist style of painting using dots, was born in 1859.

3 **Illinois Admission Day** (21st state, 1818).

6 Poet, **Joyce Kilmer**, inspired by a tree to write the lines: "I think that I shall never see/A poem as lovely as a tree," was born in 1886.

7 **The phonograph**, invented by Thomas Edison, was first demonstrated in 1877. • **Delaware Ratification Day** (1st state, 1787). • **Pearl Harbor Day** commemorates the Japanese attack on the U.S. Naval Base in 1941.

9 The **first Christmas cards** were created in England in 1842.

10 American poet, **Emily Dickinson**, was born in 1830. • Social activist, **Jane Addams**, was the first American woman to receive the Nobel Peace Prize in 1931. • **Martin Luther King, Jr.** received the Nobel Peace Prize in 1964. • **Mississippi Admission Day** (20th state, 1817).

11 **Indiana Admission Day** (19th state, 1816).

12 **Pennsylvania Ratification Day** (2nd state, 1787).

14 **Alabama Admission Day** (22nd state, 1819).

16 **Ludwig van Beethoven**, German composer, was born in 1770.

17 Charles Dickens's *A Christmas Carol* was published in 1843. • **Underdog Day** celebrates unsung heroes and the number two folks who make it possible for the number one people to succeed!

18 **New Jersey Ratification Day** (3rd state, 1787).

21 In 1620, **Pilgrims landed** in Plymouth, Massachusetts.

25 Christians celebrate the birth of Jesus Christ on **Christmas Day**.

26 **Boxing Day**, an official holiday in England and Canada, originally recognized the work of public service people, such as postal and sanitation workers. • **Kwanzaa**, which means "first fruit," is an African-American harvest celebration that lasts seven days.

28 **Iowa Admission Day** (29th state, 1846). • Ben Franklin's almanac of practical advice, *Poor Richard's Almanack*, began publication in 1732.

29 **Texas Admission Day** (28th state, 1845)

31 The Long Haul Committee dedicates today to **You're All Done Day** to recognize accomplishments of the past year. • **Make up Your Mind Day** encourages people to follow through with a decision they make today!

December Activities

Bingo Month Your class can play Bingo all year long with the **reproducible** activity on page 53. Think of 25 questions in any subject and write the answers on the Bingo board in four or five different patterns. Reproduce the various Bingo sheets and give them to your students. Give students a pile of pennies, buttons, candies, or any kind of markers. Fire away the questions until someone calls out "Bingo!"

Tell Someone They're Doing a Good Job Week is a great time to recognize people who help us every day. Ask students to design small cards in the shape of badges to give to people they appreciate. Make sure you surprise each of your students with one of the badges, too!

December 2   Georges Seurat's birthday Ask children to look at a newspaper or magazine with a magnifying glass to see that the images are made up of dots. Tell the children that a French painter, Georges Seurat, was one of the first people to see that a pattern of closely spaced dots could create an image. Hand out markers with sharp tips and ask the students to create a "dot picture."

December 17 Introduce your class to Tiny Tim in **Charles Dickens's** classic, *A Christmas Carol.* Read a chapter of this book every day until vacation.

December 21-22 Winter Solstice Explain to children that the day of the winter solstice is the shortest day and longest night of the year because of the sun's position. Point out that several holidays during this dark month—Hanukkah, Christmas, and Kwanzaa—all feature candles as part of their celebrations. Give the children the **reproducible** activity page 54. Ask the children to color the candles and write a message in the spirit of the holiday they celebrate in their own families.

December 31 You're All Done Day and **Make Up Your Mind Day** Celebrate these two New Year's Eve events ahead of time by telling students the year is done. Hooray! Tell them that on New Year's Eve they should make up their minds once and for all about something they can't decide on. Happy New Year!

Name _____   Date _____

Bingo!

Listen to your teacher call out questions. Put a marker over the right answer. Call out "Bingo!" if you cover a straight row of answers that go up and down, or across.

B I N G O

Light a Candle

December is a month of short days and long nights. Brighten someone's life by giving her or him one of these candles. Decorate each candle, and write a special message on it. Cut out the candles. Give them as holiday cards, or use them as gift tags.

JANUARY

Ring out the old, ring in the new,
Ring, happy bells, across the snow;
The year is going, let him go;
Ring out the false, ring in the true.

—from "In Memoriam,"
by Alfred, Lord Tennyson

January Is . . .

National Hobby Month   Read a New Book Month

Special Weeks in January

Spontaneous Celebrations Week (first week)
International Forgiveness Week (last full week)

Special Days in January

Inauguration Day On January 20, every four years, a U.S. president is inaugurated.
National Clean-Off-Your-Desk Day (second Monday)
Martin Luther King, Jr. Day (third Monday)
Hat Day (third Friday)
School Nurse Day (fourth Wednesday)
Chinese New Year (the eve of the second New Moon after the winter solstice)

January Events

1 **Happy New Year's Day!** • Two heroes of the Revolutionary War, **Paul Revere**, born in 1735, and flag maker, **Betsy Ross**, born in 1752, share a birthday. • This day is also the anniversary of Abraham Lincoln's **Emancipation Proclamation**, which led to the end of slavery in the United States.

2 It's **Good Luck Day** for everyone to wish each other a year's worth of fortune. • **Georgia Ratification Day** (4th state, 1788).

3 **Alaska Admission Day** (49th state, 1959).

4 Happy birthday to **Jacob Grimm**, collector and reteller of German fairy tales. • Small facts are celebrated on **Trivia Day**. • **Utah Admission Day** (45th state, 1896).

5 African-American botanist and teacher, **George Washington Carver**, died on this day in 1943.

6 **New Mexico Admission Day**, (47th state, 1912). • **Connecticut Ratification Day** (5th state, 1788).

11 In 1935, **Amelia Earhart** became the first woman pilot to fly solo across the Pacific Ocean.

12 Happy birthday to **Jack London**, American author of the classic, *Call of the Wild.*

15 Civil rights leader and Nobel Peace Prize winner, **Dr. Martin Luther King, Jr.**, was born in 1929. • **Humanitarian Day** recognizes King's contribution to the advancement of civil rights as well as the efforts of other leaders who struggled for racial equality.

16 **National Nothing Day** gives holiday revelers a breather from celebrations.

17 American founding father, statesman, and inventor, **Benjamin Franklin**, was born in 1706.

18 Happy birthday to two English authors: thesaurus author, **Peter Mark Roget**, was born in 1779, and **A.A. Milne**, author of the Winnie the Pooh books, was born in 1882.

19 American author, **Edgar Allan Poe**, was born in 1809.

21 **National Hugging Day** is a day to show affection to those near and dear.

23 **National Handwriting Day** honors **John Hancock**, the first signer of the Declaration of Independence, born in 1737. • **National Pie Day** celebrates this favorite dessert.

26 **Michigan Admission Day** (26th state, 1837).

27 Austrian composer, **Wolfgang Amadeus Mozart**, was born in 1756. • English author of *Alice's Adventures in Wonderland*, **Lewis Carroll**, was born in 1832.

28 The **National Day of Excellence** recognizes the importance of superior effort and achievement.

29 **Kansas Admission Day** (34th state, 1861).

January Activities

National Hobby Month Announce a Hobby Fair for this month. Encourage those who want to participate to prepare a flier or poster that tells interested students how to get started in a hobby or how to begin a collection. Set aside time for students with hobbies to talk about them informally before the class.

School Nurse Day Have your students create and send a special thank-you poster to the school nurse. Ask one student to paint a big red cross, the first aid sign, on a white piece of posterboard or construction paper. Then give each child a small bandage on which to write a special thank-you message to stick on the poster.

January 1 After vacation, celebrate a belated birthday for Paul Revere by reading Henry Wadsworth Longfellow's "Paul Revere's Ride."

January 4 Remember **Jacob Grimm's birthday** by reading his fairy tale, *Snow White*, which begins on a snowy winter day. It's also **Trivia Day**. Ask students to provide trivia questions in any area. Ask them to write each question on one side of an index card with the answer on the other. Use the cards to hold a blitz session of the trivia game your class created.

January 15 Honor the memory of **Dr. Martin Luther King, Jr.** by reading his famous "I Have a Dream" speech. Ask the children to share their dreams for a better world. Then have them complete **reproducible** activity page 58.

January 19 In honor of **Edgar Allan Poe's birthday**, dim the classroom lights and read aloud Poe's famous poem, "The Raven."

January 23 is **National Pie Day**, which celebrates a wonderful dessert. On this day, bring in a few pies to teach your class about fractions. First, draw some pies on the chalkboard, and give children the chance to divide them into halves, quarters, and eighths. Hand out **reproducible** activity page 59 to give students plenty of practice in handling fractions. When you are confident that students understand the concept of fractions, cut into the tasty pies and enjoy.

Name _____   Date _____

I Have a Dream

Do you have a dream for a better world? Write about your dream in the dream cloud below.

Name _____   Date _____

And You Shall Have Some Pie

Here are some delicious pies. Can you cut them into pieces for some pie lovers?
Read the problems, then divide each pie into the correct sections.

1. Eight hungry guests all
want pie. Give them each an
equal piece.

2. There are four guests. Divide the pie
into fourths. Only one guest wants pie
right away. If you take out one piece,
how many fourths are left? _____

3. There are six guests, but only two are hungry
for pie now. Divide the pie into six pieces. If you
take out two, how many sixths of the pie are left? _____

FEBRUARY

The February sunshine steeps your boughs,
And tints the buds and swells the leaves within.

—from "Twenty-Second of February,"
by William Cullen Bryant

BE MY VALENTINE

February Is . . .

Afro-American History Month   American Heart Month
National Children's Dental Health Month
National Grapefruit Month

Special Weeks in February

National New Idea Week (first full week) Creativity and problem solving
are promoted during this week.

Special Days in February

Presidents' Day (third Monday in February) The February birthdays of George
Washington and Abraham Lincoln are celebrated on this day.

February Events

1 It's **Be an Encourager® Day**, the perfect time to offer heartfelt encouragement to fellow students, friends, and family. • **Freedom Day** commemorates Abraham Lincoln's approval, in 1865, of the 13th Constitutional Amendment outlawing slavery. • African-American poet, **Langston Hughes**, was born in 1902. • The **U.S. Supreme Court** convened for the first time in 1790.

2 On **Groundhog Day** everyone waits to see if the groundhog sees his shadow, meaning six weeks of winter remain.

4 Aviation hero **Charles Augustus Lindbergh**, who flew the first non-stop solo flight across the Atlantic, was born in 1902.

6 **Ronald Reagan**, 40th president of the United States, was born in 1911. • *Curious George*, H.A. Rey's frisky monkey, first appeared in print in 1939. • **Massachusetts Ratification Day** (6th state, 1788).

7 **Laura Ingalls Wilder**, author of the heartwarming family stories of the American frontier, the Little House books, was born in 1867.

9 The United States established the first **U.S. Weather Bureau** in 1870.

11 American inventor of the electric lamp, phonograph, and components of much of today's technology, **Thomas Alva Edison**, was born in 1847.

12 The 16th president of the United States and emancipator of the slaves, **Abraham Lincoln**, was born in 1809.

14 **Ferris Wheel Day** honors the 1859 birth of American engineer, George Ferris, who designed the first Ferris wheel for an exposition in 1893. • **Read to Your Child Day** encourages adults to read aloud to children to develop a child's early love of books. • **Valentine's Day** is an unofficial, but widely celebrated, day of affection. • It's also **National Have-a-Heart Day**, which promotes good nutrition and exercise to build healthy hearts. • **Arizona Admission Day** (48th state, 1912). • **Oregon Admission Day** (33rd state, 1859).

15 **Galileo Galilei**, Italian astronomer and physicist who reasoned that falling objects of different weights would land at the same time, was born in 1564.

19 **Nicolaus Copernicus**, the Polish astronomer who first recognized that the sun was at the center of our solar system, was born in 1473.

22 Revolutionary War general and the first president of the United States, **George Washington**, was born in 1732.

24 Folklorist and brother of Jacob Grimm, **Wilhelm Carl Grimm**, was born in Germany in 1786.

25 **Pierre Auguste Renoir**, French Impressionist painter, was born in 1841.

27 American poet, **Henry Wadsworth Longfellow**, was born in 1807.

29 Every four years it's **Leap Year Day**, which means a day is added to the calendar to account for the extra time it takes the Earth to revolve around the sun each year: 365 days, 5 hours, 48 minutes, and approximately 45 seconds.

February Activities

National Children's Dental Health Month
Invite a dental hygienist or dentist to class to demonstrate proper tooth-brushing techniques and answer students' questions about their teeth.

National New Idea Week is a great time to solicit ideas about how to change the same old routines. Have the students brainstorm some new ideas for solving those ongoing school annoyances: crowded hallways and staircases, long lunchroom lines, overly popular gym and playground equipment, or other knotty problems.

Presidents' Day Ask students to write a letter to the President, in which they suggest what they would do if they could be president for a day. Send the batch of letters to the White House!

February 2 It's **Groundhog Day**! At lunch or recess, take your students outside to see if they can see their shadows. Explain that, according to legend, if the groundhog emerges from his winter hiding place and sees his shadow, there will be six more weeks of winter. Will the groundhog see his shadow today?

February 9 Commemorate the founding of the **U.S. Weather Bureau** by having the children write a recipe for a perfect day. See **reproducible** activity page 64. Have them list their ingredients on the left side and the "cooking" steps on the right. Set aside time for a perfect day "cooking" class when children can read their cards aloud. Wind up the activity by reading about a hilarious experience in *Cloudy With a Chance of Meatballs*, by Judith Barrett.

February 14 Provide a secret **Valentine** box in the classroom in which children can place their "heart halves." See **reproducible** activity page 63. Open the box and hand out a half of a heart to each child. Then ask the children to find who has the other half.

February 19 Celebrate the sun on the birthday of **Nicolaus Copernicus**. Explain to the class that Copernicus was the first astronomer to insist that the sun, not the Earth, was the center of our solar system. Read books about the planets , and show the class pictures of how they orbit the sun.

February 29 Whether or not **Leap Year Day** is celebrated this year, ask students to write about what they would do with an extra bonus day.

Half Hearted Fun

Decorate and write a Valentine message across both sides of this heart. Cut out the entire heart, then cut it again along the broken line. Put one half of the heart in a Valentine box and keep the other half for yourself. Try to find your "secret valentine" by matching the half hearts.

Name _____ Date _____

Recipe For a Perfect Day

What would the weather be like if you could "cook up" a perfect day? Write the ingredients on one side of the recipe card and the steps for mixing them on the other side.

RECIPE FOR A PERFECT DAY

Ingredients	Steps
_____	_____
_____	_____
_____	_____
_____	_____
_____	_____
_____	_____

MARCH

O wind a-blowing all day long,
O wind, that sings so loud a song!
—*from "The Wind,"*
by Robert Louis Stevenson

March Is . . .

American Red Cross Month
Music in Our Schools Month
National Women's History Month
Youth Art Month

Foot Health Month
National Peanut Month
Poetry Month

Special Weeks in March

Return the Borrowed Books Week (first full week)
Newspaper Education Week (first full week)

Special Days in March

Easter A Christian holiday observed on a Sunday between March 22 and April 25. Easter celebrates the resurrection of Jesus Christ.

Passover An eight-day Jewish feast observed in March or April. Passover celebrates the exodus from Egypt, when the Israelites became free from slavery.

Purim A joyous Jewish holiday observed in March or April, celebrating the heroism of the beautiful Queen Esther, who saved her people from an evil plot to destroy them.

Plant a Flower Day Second Sunday in March

The first day of spring falls on March 20 or 21.

March Events

1   **Nebraska Admission Day** (37th state, 1867). • **Ohio Admission Day** (17th state, 1803).

2   Theodor Seuss Geisel, better known as **Dr. Seuss**, was born in 1904. *The Cat in the Hat, Green Eggs and Ham,* and *The Lorax* are among the best-loved books by this legendary children's author.

3   **I Want You to Be Happy Day** is dedicated to thoughtfulness towards others. • **Alexander Graham Bell**, inventor of the telephone, was born in Edinburgh, Scotland in 1847. • **Florida Admission Day** (27th state, 1845).

4   **Vermont Admission Day** (14th state, 1791).

5   **Crispus Attucks Day** honors the runaway slave who, on this date in 1770, was the first to give his life for American independence.

6   **Alamo Day** commemorates the day in 1836 when 187 heroic Texans (Davy Crockett may have been one of them.) died fighting for independence from Mexico. "Remember the Alamo" later became the battle cry of Sam Houston's forces who defeated the Mexicans at San Jacinto on April 21.

7   **Janet Guthrie**, the first female race-car driver to qualify for the Indianapolis 500, was born in 1938.

8   **International Women's Day** honors all women, but especially working women all over the world.

9   **Amerigo Vespucci**, the Italian explorer who reached the coast of South America between 1499 and 1502, was born in 1451.

10   **Alexander Graham Bell** transmitted the **first telephone message** in 1876. • **Harriet Tubman**, heroic Underground Railroad leader, died on this day in 1913.

12   The **United States Post Office** was established in 1789. • In 1912, Juliet Low founded **Girl Scouts of the USA**.

13   **Uranus**, the seventh planet from the sun, was discovered by astronomer Sir William Herschel in 1781.

14   **Albert Einstein** was born in Ulm, Germany in 1879.

15   **Maine Admission Day** (23rd state, 1820).

16   **James Madison**, fourth president of the United States, was born in 1751.

17   **St. Patrick's Day** commemorates the patron saint of Ireland.

20   Happy birthday to *Sesame Street's* **Big Bird**!

21   German composer **Johann Sebastian Bach** was born in 1685.

22   **National Goof-Off Day** is a day to relax and just have some fun. • In 1972, the Senate passed and submitted the **Equal Rights Amendment** for ratification by the states.

23   On **Liberty Day**, we remember Patrick Henry's stirring words to the Virginian colonists in 1775: "...give me liberty or give me death."

25   **Global Understanding Day** draws attention to the need for understanding among peoples of the world.

26   It's **Make Up Your Own Holiday Day**. Anything goes! • American poet **Robert Frost** was born in 1874.

30   We honor America's physicians on **Doctors' Day**.

31   **Rene Descartes**, French philosopher and mathematician, was born in 1596. • **Franz Joseph Haydn**, "father of the symphony," was born in 1732.

March Activities

National Peanut Month
Most everyone likes peanuts. But do the children know that peanuts are seeds? Each child in the class can grow his or her own peanut plant. Soak shelled, raw peanuts in cold water overnight. The following day, the students can plant their peanuts in paper cups filled with soil. Place the cups in a sunny place and keep the soil moist. The first green sprouts will appear within a week to ten days.

Newspaper Education Week Start a class newspaper. Appoint reporters, interviewers, columnists, sportswriters, editors, artists—even photographers. Have the "staff" work in groups to plan their newspaper and cover the news as it "breaks" in your class, school, and community.

March 2 Celebrate **Dr. Seuss's** birthday by reading to the children some favorites by this beloved children's author. See if the children can make up some wacky "Seussian" rhymes of their own.

March 3 I Want You To Be Happy Day is a great opportunity to get the children thinking about the feelings of others. Ask them to write their names on index cards or slips of paper. Put all the names into a box, and have each child pick a name without telling anyone whose it is. Then give students a few minutes to think of something nice to do for the people they picked—tell the person three things you like about her or him; invite the person to play with you; share something; tell the person a story; draw a picture or make something to give the person as a gift. See **reproducible** activity page 69.

March 8   On International Women's Day, invite a woman from your community—maybe the mother of one of your students—to talk to the class about her job. Encourage all the children to talk about what they might like to do when they grow up.

March 10 Celebrate the transmission of the **first telephone message** by practicing telephone manners. You'll need two toy telephones placed at opposite sides of the room. Or let the children make their own paper-cup phones.

March 12 Take the class on a trip to your local **post office**. In advance, arrange to have a postal worker talk to the children about how mail is picked up from boxes, sorted, and delivered to its destination. Back in the classroom, talk about the pictures on stamps. Then invite the children to design their own postage stamps.

March 13 On the anniversary of the discovery of the planet **Uranus**, have the children make a human model of the solar system. One student can be the sun, while the others whirl and twirl in their "orbits." (The order of planets from the sun is as follows: Mercury, Venus, Earth, Mars, Jupiter, Saturn, Uranus, Neptune, Pluto.) Two or three children can hold hands to make rings around Jupiter, Saturn, and Uranus, and a single child can circle the earth as the moon.

March 17 On **St. Patrick's Day**, tell the children the Irish folk belief that there's a pot of gold at the end of the rainbow. Then show them how real rainbows occur. Make a rainbow on the wall with a prism, if you have one available. You can also angle a small mirror in a glass baking dish half-filled with water, then shine a strong flashlight at the part of the mirror that is under water. A small rainbow will appear on a sheet of white paper held opposite the mirror. (Helpful hints: darken the room, use opaque paper, adjust the position of the flashlight.)

March 26 Children will love **Make Up Your Own Holiday Day**. Invite them to think up names for holidays to celebrate their favorite things or activities. Then have them make cards for their new holidays and send them to friends. Older children will enjoy hearing and illustrating **Robert Frost's** well-known poem, "Stopping by Woods on a Snowy Evening."

March 31 To celebrate the birthday of **Franz Joseph Haydn**, play a recording of the beginning of the second movement of Haydn's *Surprise Symphony*. Challenge the children to listen for the loud chord that is meant to surprise the audience. Then invite them to make up their own words to the theme. (It sounds a bit like "Twinkle, Twinkle Little Star.")

Happy "I Want You To Be Happy Day"

Help someone feel happy. Think of three nice things to say to the person. Fill in this card, and draw a picture. Then cut out the card and give it to someone for "I Want You To Be Happy Day." (Don't forget to sign your message at the bottom. Write your name, or sign your card, "Your Mystery Friend.")

Dear _____ ,

Here are three things I really like about you.

1. _____

2. _____

3. _____

I hope you're feeling happy today!

_____

APRIL

I wandered lonely as a cloud
That floats on high o'er vales and hills,
When all at once I saw a crowd,
A host of golden daffodils...

—*from "Daffodils,"*
by William Wordsworth

April Is . . .

International Guitar Month   Keep America Beautiful Month
Mathematics Education Month   Month of the Young Child
National Garden Month   National Humor Month

Special Weeks in April

National Library Week (dates vary)
National Bike Safety Week (usually the third full week)
National Volunteer Week (third full week)
National Week of the Ocean (third full week)

Special Days in April

Easter A Christian holiday celebrated on a Sunday between March 22 and April 25 (see March).

Passover An eight-day Jewish feast celebrated in March or April (see March).

Purim A Jewish holiday celebrated in March or April (see March).

Patriot's Day The third Monday in April commemorates the Battle of Lexington and Concord in 1775.

April Events

1 It's **April Fools' Day!** Better watch out—and have a few tricks up your own sleeve.

2 **International Children's Book Day** commemorates the birth of author **Hans Christian Andersen** in Copenhagen, Denmark in 1805, and honors all children's authors.

3 **Washington Irving**, the creator of *Rip Van Winkle*, was born in New York City in 1783.

4 The nation mourned when the great civil rights leader **Dr. Martin Luther King, Jr.** was assassinated in 1968.

5 African-American educator, author, and leader **Booker T. Washington** was born in Virginia in 1856.

6 In 1896, the first modern **Olympic Games** took place in Athens, Greece.

7 **World Health Day** commemorates the establishment of the World Health Organization in 1948.

8 In Japan, the **Buddha's birthday** is celebrated with a flower festival (*Hana Matsuri* in Japanese).

9 The **first public library** in the United States opened in 1833, in Peterborough, New Hampshire. • At 1:30 PM at Appomattox Court House, Virginia, in 1865, General Robert E. Lee surrendered to General Ulysses S. Grant, marking the end of the **Civil War**.

10 The **American Society for the Prevention of Cruelty to Animals** was chartered in 1866.

11 The **Civil Rights Act of 1968** was signed into law by President Lyndon B. Johnson.

12 Favorite children's author **Beverly Cleary**, best known for her characters Beezus and Ramona Quimby and Henry Huggins, was born in 1916.

13 The third president of the United States and author of the Declaration of Independence, **Thomas Jefferson**, was born in 1743.

14 **Pan American Day** celebrates friendship and cooperation among all American countries. • In 1865, President **Abraham Lincoln** was shot by John Wilkes Booth. He died the following day.

15 Today is **Rubber Eraser Day**. In 1770, an English chemist, Joseph Priestley, discovered that latex could rub out pencil marks.

16 Celebrated comedian **Charlie Chaplin** was born in London, England, in 1889. • Aviation pioneer **Wilbur Wright** was born in 1867.

18 In 1775, **Paul Revere** made his famous "midnight ride" from Boston to Concord to warn the American patriots of the approaching British.

22 "Give Earth a Chance" is the motto for **Earth Day**, dedicated to preserving a clean living environment.

23 England's venerated bard, **William Shakespeare,** was born in Stratford-on-Avon, England in 1564. He died on the same date in 1616.

27 **Samuel F.B. Morse**, best known for inventing the telegraph and creating the International Morse Code, was born in 1791. • Civil rights leader **Coretta Scott King** was born in 1927.

28 **Maryland Ratification Day** (7th state, 1788).

29 What would we do without zippers? The **zipper** was patented in 1913.

30 **Hamburgers** were first introduced at the St. Louis World's Fair in 1904. • **Louisiana Admission Day** (18th state, 1812).

April Activities

Mathematics Education Month Plan some out-of-the-ordinary math games to do with your class this month. For younger children, set up rows of jelly beans in repeated color sequences and see if students can detect and continue the pattern. "Cookie Math" is a great game for students learning multiplication. The first roll of a die tells how many cookies (circles) the player should draw. The second roll determines the number of chips (dots) to draw on each cookie. How many chips? Count the dots on one cookie and multiply by the total number of cookies. How many chips in all?

Month of the Young Child
Boost students' self esteem by making sure everyone in the class gets an award this month. Make badges that say, "All-Around Super Kid," "Class Poet," "A+ Helper," "Science Whiz," "Math Genius," and so on.

National Volunteer Week Discuss the satisfaction to be gained from working just to help other people. Then plan some volunteer work the children could do—help a neighbor with yardwork or housework, offer to do an errand for a busy family member, participate in a local charity drive.

April 1 Here's a silly trick you can play on the children in your class. Challenge them to spell any word. (The correct spelling of "any word" is A N Y W O R D!) Then invite them to write a story beginning with, "Wait until you hear what happened to me on the way to school." Have them continue with the wildest, craziest events they can imagine, then end the story with, **"April Fool!"**

April 4 Here are some books for your students to read about the life and words of **Dr. Martin Luther King, Jr.** *A Picture Book of Martin Luther King, Jr.*, David A. Adler, Holiday House, 1989; *Let Freedom Ring: A Ballad of Martin Luther King, Jr.*, Myra Cohn Livingston, Holiday House, 1992; *Young Martin Luther King, Jr. "I Have a Dream,"* Troll, 1992.

April 7 Getting exercise is important for good health. On **World Health Day**, set up an exercise course with 5 stations around the classroom. Leave instructions and necessary equipment at each station: Do 5 jumping jacks. Run 20 steps in place. Skip rope 10 times. Lift a stack of books. Jump over a carton.

April 14 On **Pan American Day**, have the students make flags of the Americas to decorate the classroom. (Full-color pictures of the flags can be found in the *World Book* encyclopedia under the entry, "flags.") Also, locate the countries of the North and South American continents on a map.

April 15 In appreciation of the invention of the **rubber eraser**, challenge the students to get through a whole day without using an eraser. By the end of the day, they'll all want to say a big "thank you" to Joseph Priestley, the inventor of this useful item.

April 16 **Charlie Chaplin** became famous as a star of silent movies—before "talkies" were invented. Challenge the class to ten minutes of silence. During that time, they'll have to express their thoughts and feelings by actions only—no words allowed!

April 22 On **Earth Day**, choose an area near your school that could use beautification, and have a flower-planting party. If you have a camera on hand, take "before" and "after" pictures of your area. Take pictures of the children working and send them to your local newspaper, or post them on the bulletin board. Then invite your children to celebrate Earth Day in original poems. See **reproducible** activity page 74.

April 27 Show the students how to use a flashlight to send **Morse Code** messages. (A flashlight with a flash button will work best.) Students should count to three between letters and five between words. See **reproducible** activity page 75. Invite the children to make up their own secret codes using letters, numbers, or symbols.

Name _____   Date _____

My Poem for Earth Day

Think about your favorite place on earth. Is it the ocean...a quiet place in the woods...a beautiful meadow...your own backyard? Do you go there to think...to play...to daydream...to dance? Think about what your favorite place is like and what you do there. Then fill in the blanks. Make up a last line for your poem. Give your poem a title. Draw a picture to go with your poem.

_____

_____ **is my favorite place.**

I go there to _____ .

I go there to _____ .

I go there to _____

_____ .

Name _____   Date _____

Dots and Dashes

Decide on a short message to send to the class in International Morse Code. First, write your message in words. Then write your message in Morse Code.

International Morse Code

A	• —	**J**	• — — —	**S**	• • •
B	— • • •	**K**	— • —	**T**	—
C	— • — •	**L**	• — • •	**U**	• • —
D	— • •	**M**	— —	**V**	• • • —
E	•	**N**	— •	**W**	• — —
F	• • — •	**O**	— — —	**X**	— • • —
G	— — •	**P**	• — — •	**Y**	— • — —
H	• • • •	**Q**	— — • —	**Z**	— — • •
I	• •	**R**	• — •		

Write your message in words here. _____

_____

_____

_____

Write your message in Morse Code here. _____

_____

_____

_____

MAY

All roads may meet at the world's end,
But, hey for the heart of May!
Come, choose your road and away, dear lad,
Come, choose your road and away.

—*from "The Call of the Spring,"
by Alfred Noyes*

May Is . . .

American Bike Month
Correct Posture Month

Better Sleep Month
Older Americans Month

Special Weeks in May

Be Kind to Animals Week (first full week)
Cartoon Art Appreciation Week (first full week)
National Raisin Week (first full week)
National Wildflower Week (first full week)
National Police Week (second full week)

Special Days in May

Mother's Day We honor all mothers on the second Sunday in May.

Victoria Day In Canada, Queen Victoria's birthday (May 24) is celebrated on the first Monday preceding May 25.

Armed Forces Day Men and women who have served in the armed forces are honored on the third Saturday in May.

Memorial Day On the last Monday in May, we remember and honor those who have died, especially those who gave their lives in battle.

1 **Lei Day** is a gala Hawaiian festival that includes music, dancing, and the crowning of the Lei Day Queen.

4 It's **National Teacher Day**—a day to honor those who not only instruct, but inspire, motivate, and guide our next generation of Americans. (That's you!)

5 On **Cinco de Mayo** (Fifth of May), Mexicans everywhere celebrate with parades and festivals General Ignacio Zaragoza's victory over invading French forces in 1862. • **Nelly Bly** (Elizabeth Cochrane Seaman), American journalist and fighter for women's rights, was born in 1867. • Poet **Gwendolyn Brooks**, first African-American to receive a Pulitzer Prize, was born in 1917. • On this date in 1961, **Alan Shepard, Jr.** became the first American in space.

7 This date is the birthday of English poet **Robert Browning** (1812), German composer **Johannes Brahms** (1833), and the Russian composer of "The Nutcracker," **Peter Ilyich Tchaikovsky** (1840).

8 The **first U.S. patent for an automobile** was awarded to G.B. Selden in 1879.

9 Abolitionist leader **John Brown** was born in 1800. • **James M. Barrie**, creator of Peter Pan, was born in 1860.

11 **Irving Berlin**, the songwriter who gave us "Alexander's Ragtime Band," "White Christmas," "God Bless America," and many other all-time favorites, was born in Russia in 1888. • **Minnesota Admission Day** (32nd state, 1858).

12 It's **Limerick Day**, in honor of **Edward Lear**, English poet born in 1812, best remembered for his light verse.

15 **L. Frank Baum**, author of *The Wonderful Wizard of Oz*, was born in 1856.

16 Happy birthday to Oscar! The very first **Academy Awards** presentations took place on this date in 1929.

18 It's **International Museum Day**—a great day for a class trip. • This date marks the eruption of **Mount St. Helens** volcano in the state of Washington in 1980.

19 Civil rights activist **Malcolm X**, originally Malcolm Little, was born in Omaha, Nebraska in 1925.

20 In 1927, **Captain Charles Lindbergh** boarded the *Spirit of St. Louis* to make the first solo trans-Atlantic flight in history. • On this same date in 1932, **Amelia Earhart** became the first woman to fly solo across the Atlantic.

21 The **American Red Cross** was founded in 1881 by Clara Barton.

22 English physician **Sir Arthur Conan Doyle**, creator of detective character Sherlock Holmes, was born in Edinburgh, Scotland, in 1859.

23 **Mary Cassatt**, an American artist noted for her impressionistic scenes of family life, was born in 1844. • **South Carolina Ratification Day** (8th state, 1788).

24 The **Brooklyn Bridge**, connecting the New York City boroughs of Manhattan and Brooklyn, was opened in 1883. Designed by John A. Roebling, it is considered a work of art as well as a remarkable feat of engineering.

25 In honor of **Bill "Bojangles" Robinson**, born in 1878 and known as "The King of Tap Dancers," this date is designated **National Tap Dance Day**.

26 **Dr. Sally Kristen Ride**, first American woman in space, was born in Encino, California in 1951.

29 **John Fitzgerald Kennedy**, 35th president of the United States was born in 1917. • **Wisconsin Admission Day** (30th state, 1848). • **Rhode Island Ratification Day** (13th state, 1790).

American Bike Month Have a bike in the classroom. Turn it upside down, turn the pedals by hand, and let the students see what happens. How do the pedals make the wheel turn? What does the chain do? What about the gears? Talk about other uses for that invention of all inventions—the wheel. Share with the students that the first bicycles had no pedals. The rider had to push the bike along with his or her feet!

National Wildflower Week Everyone knows that flowers grow from seeds we plant in the ground. But how do wildflowers grow? Explain that seeds of flowers and trees are carried in many ways—by the wind, by streams, and by animals that have fur for the seeds to stick to. Then go outdoors to find wildflowers. If you have a field guide, you might try some identifications. Advise students not to pick the flowers—it's better to leave them for everyone to enjoy. See **reproducible** activity page 80.

Mother's Day Encourage the children to *really* talk to their moms. Here are some questions they might ask: What did you look like when you were my age? What did you like to do? Who were your friends? What was school like then? How did you decide what you would do when you grew up? What are your plans for the future? Students could tape their interviews—then write them up and illustrate them with drawings or photos of their moms, then and now. See **reproducible** activity page 81.

May 1 On **Lei Day**, have a Hawaiian festival. Show the children how to make their own leis with pastel-colored tissue-paper flowers held together with pipe cleaners. Decorate the room with paper flowers, too. Play Hawaiian music, and let the children try doing the *hula*. Serve canned or fresh pineapple as a snack. Everyone should wear bright colors and say *Aloha* to mean "Greetings," or "Hello."

May 4 It's **National Teacher Day**. Tell your students you want to let them know that you appreciate them just as you like to know that they appreciate you. Maybe you can exchange "thank-you" cards with your class.

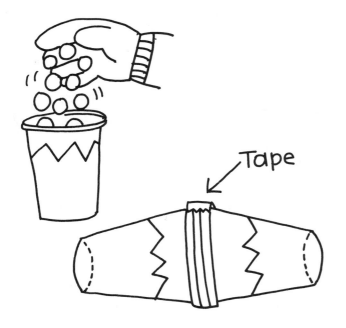

Tape

May 5 Tell the children that **Cinco de Mayo** means the fifth of May in Spanish. See if they can learn to count to ten in Spanish (uno, dos, tres, cuatro, cinco, seis, siete, ocho, nueve, diez), and learn the names of the other months, too (enero, febrero, marzo, abril, mayo, junio, julio, agosto, septiembre, octubre, noviembre, diciembre). Hold your own Cinco de Mayo festival with Mexican food, music, and games. Make a piñata and paper cup *maracas*. Learn the Mexican Hat Dance.

May 8 To commemorate the **first U.S. patent for an automobile**, explain that a government patent allows an inventor to prevent others from making or selling his invention. To receive a patent, an invention must be both original and useful. Challenge your students to come up with pictures or descriptions of their own inventions. A better way to keep dry in the rain? An automatic dog walker? A new and wonderful toy?

May 12 Read aloud some funny poems from **Edward Lear's** *Book of Nonsense*, and "The Owl and the Pussycat," as well as some of his limericks. Can the children make up limericks of their own?

May 15 Everyone loves *The Wonderful Wizard of Oz* by **L. Frank Baum**, but many children think this classic began as a movie! Read aloud from the book, sharing the illustrations with the children. How do they think the book compares with the movie?

May 23 In an art book from the library, show the students some color prints of paintings by **Mary Cassatt**. Talk about the colors she used and the subjects of her paintings. Invite the children to draw or paint scenes from their own family lives.

May 24 Show the class a picture of the **Brooklyn Bridge**. Then do the following activity to demonstrate how a suspension bridge works. Ask two volunteers to hold the ends of a length of string so that there is just a little slack. Tie a shorter length of string at each end. Make a slip knot in the bottom of each shorter string, and slip the ends of a yardstick through the loops. For realism, roll a toy car or truck along the yardstick. Explain that if this were a real bridge over a river, the two students would be metal supports, and the strings steel cables.

Name _____   Date _____

Flower Power

Here are three wildflowers:

1. Violet   **2. Black-eyed Susan**   **3. Lupine**

Find each flower in the picture below. Write its number on the line below the flower. Then color by number.

Use purple for 1.   Use yellow for 2.   Use pink for 3.

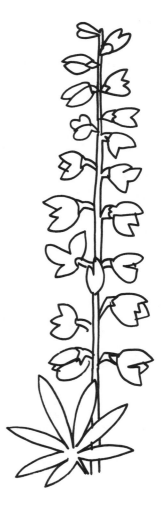

_____   _____   _____

Name _____   Date _____

My Mom

Write about your mother. What is she like now? What was she like when she was your age? At the bottom of the page, draw pictures or paste photos showing how your mom looked when she was a kid and how she looks now.

_____

_____

_____

_____

_____

_____

_____

_____

JUNE

And what is so rare as a day in June?
Then, if ever, come perfect days...

*—from "The Vision of Sir Launfal,"
by James Russell Lowell*

June is . . .

American Rivers Month
National Fresh Fruit and Vegetable Month
Zoo and Aquarium Month

Special Weeks in June

National Little League Baseball Week (begins the second Monday in June)

Special Days in June

National Spelling Bee Finals On Wednesday and Thursday of Memorial Day week, the "Spelling Olympics" are held in Washington, D.C.

Father's Day We honor all fathers on the third Sunday in June.

The First Day of Summer falls on June 20 or 21.

1 **Kentucky Admission Day** (15th state, 1792). • **Tennessee Admission Day** (16th state, 1796).

3 Ernest L. Thayer's well-loved comic baseball poem, "**Casey at the Bat**," first appeared in the *San Francisco Examiner* in 1888.

5 The **first hot-air balloon flight** took place in France in 1783. Joseph and Jacques Montgolfier's balloon flew for ten minutes, rising 1,500 feet and going 7,500 feet before landing. • **Robert F. Kennedy** was assassinated in Los Angeles in 1968 while campaigning for the Democratic presidential nomination. Sirhan Sirhan was convicted of the crime.

6 **D-Day**, the 1944 landing of the Allied Expeditionary Force in Normandy, France, was a turning point in World War II. • **Nathan Hale**, Revolutionary War hero, was born in 1755. His celebrated final words before being hanged by the British for espionage, were: "I only regret that I have but one life to lose for my country." • In 1872 **Susan B. Anthony** led women to the polls in Rochester, New York, and was fined for voting.

7 In 1767, frontiersman **Daniel Boone** supposedly first saw the land which would become Kentucky.

8 James Madison proposed the **Bill of Rights**, the first ten amendments to the U.S. Constitution, in 1789.

9 **Cole Porter**, celebrated American songwriter, was born in 1893.

10 **Hattie McDaniel**, first African-American actress to win an Academy Award (for her role in *Gone With the Wind*), was born in 1889. • Beloved children's author and illustrator **Maurice Sendak** was born in 1928.

11 **Jeannette Rankin**, the first woman elected to Congress, was born in 1880.

12 In 1839, **Abner Doubleday** invented America's favorite pastime—**baseball**.

13 Civil Rights leader **Medgar Evers** was assassinated in 1963. His death spurred the passage of a comprehensive civil rights law.

14 **Flag Day** celebrates the adoption in 1777 of the stars and stripes as the flag of the United States. • **Harriet Beecher Stowe**, the author of *Uncle Tom's Cabin*, was born in 1811. Her book became a focal point in the campaign against slavery. • **Burl Ives**, actor and folk singer, was born in 1909.

15 **Arkansas Admission Day** (25th state, 1836).

16 Russian cosmonaut Valentina V. Tereshkova became the **first woman in space** in 1963.

17 Father **Jacques Marquette** and **Louis Joliet** discovered the Mississippi River in 1673. • **Igor Stravinsky**, major twentieth-century composer, was born in Russia in 1882.

20 **West Virginia Admission Day** (35th state, 1863).

21 **New Hampshire Ratification Day** (9th state, 1788).

22 **Anne Morrow Lindbergh**, noted American writer (*Gift from the Sea*) and aviator, was born in 1907.

25 The **Battle of Little Big Horn** was fought in 1876. Sioux Indians, led by Chiefs Sitting Bull and Crazy Horse, overwhelmed an entire force commanded by Lt. Col. George Armstrong Custer. • **Virginia Ratification Day** (10th state, 1788).

27 Sing "Happy Birthday to You" to the composer of "Happy Birthday to You"—**Mildred J. Hill**, born in 1859. • **Helen Keller** was born in 1880. Blind and deaf from the age of 19 months, she became a prolific writer and advocate for the blind.

June Activities

National Fresh Fruit and Vegetable Month What's the difference between a fruit and a vegetable? Answer this question once and for all. *All* plants are vegetables. A fruit is the part of a plant that contains *seeds*. That means that a green pepper, a tomato, an apple, and a peach are all fruits. Carrots and beets are roots. Lettuce and spinach are leaves. Slice open some vegetables to show which ones have seeds inside. Then have a vegetable *smorgasbord*. Encourage the students to taste some raw fruits and vegetables that may be new to them, such as turnip or mango. See **reproducible** activity page 85.

Father's Day The traditional Father's Day gifts are always fun to make—clay hand-print paperweights, pencil holders, bookmarks, picture frames, and original cards. For children who want to give their dads something unusual—and useful—suggest coupon books. Children cut strips of construction paper and staple them together. Then they write on each strip something they might do for their fathers: help with yardwork, wash the dishes, do an errand, set the table, wash the car, help with the cooking, straighten up a storage room or closet, take out the trash, walk the dog on a rainy day.

June 6 Pass around a **Susan B. Anthony** silver dollar, if you have one. Then talk about the importance of equal voting rights for all.

June 8 Discuss the **Bill of Rights** with the class. Encourage the children to draw up a children's Bill of Rights.

June 12 Happy birthday to baseball! Play ball. Hand out **reproducible** activity page 86 just for fun.

June 14 Talk about the symbolism of the **American Flag**. The thirteen stripes stand for the original thirteen colonies, and the fifty stars for the fifty states of the Union. The color red stands for courage, white for liberty, and blue for justice. Invite the students to design a class flag with figures and colors that represent class values and qualities. Children might also create flags to represent themselves, their families, or their neighborhoods.

Name _____   Date _____

Have a Slice

Every picture on this page is a fruit. When you cut a fruit in slices you can see the seeds inside. Match each slice with the fruit it came from.

Name _____   Date _____

Batty Baseball

There are seven silly things going on in this picture. Can you find them?

JULY

A boat, beneath a sunny sky,
Lingering onward dreamily
In an evening of July...

—*from "Through the Looking Glass,"
by Lewis Carroll*

July Is . . .

Anti-Boredom Month
National Recreation and Parks Month

National Hot Dog Month
Read an "Almanac" Month

Special Weeks in July

Music for Life Week (first full week)
Space Week (third full week)

Special Days in July

National Ice Cream Day It's easy to see why this day is celebrated during
the hottest time of the year—the third Sunday in July.

July Events

1 The **Battle of Gettysburg** began in 1863. A turning point in the Civil War, the three-day battle was a decisive victory for the Union. • **Canada Day** (formerly Dominion Day) is celebrated with picnics, parades, and sports events to commemorate the union of the provinces into the Dominion of Canada in 1867.

2 The **Civil Rights Act of 1964** was passed, barring discrimination on the basis of race. • **Thurgood Marshall**, first African-American Justice of the Supreme Court, was born in 1908.

3 **Idaho Admission Day** (43rd state, 1890).

4 **"America the Beautiful"** was published in 1895. • **Louis Armstrong**, jazz immortal, was born in 1900. • **Independence Day** celebrates the adoption of the Declaration of Independence by the Continental Congress in 1776.

5 **Phineas T. Barnum** was born in 1810. His circus survives as part of the Ringling Brothers and Barnum & Bailey Circus.

6 Peter Rabbit, Jemima Puddleduck, and Tom Kitten are only a few of the many beloved animal characters created by **Beatrix Potter**, born in London in 1866.

7 The beautiful paintings of **Marc Chagall**, who was born in Russia in 1887, are loved for their brilliant colors and fanciful scenes.

9 The **Vermont Quilt Festival** is held on this day each year.

10 **Wyoming Admission Day** (44th state, 1890).

11 **Special Recreation Day** focuses attention on the recreational rights and needs of disabled people.

14 **Bastille Day**, the French Independence Day, is celebrated with fireworks and festivals. On this date in 1789, French revolutionaries freed the prisoners in the Bastille, the prison that was, for them, a symbol of injustice. • **Woody Guthrie**, American composer of more than a thousand folk songs, was born in 1912.

17 **Muñoz-Rivera Day**, a public holiday in Puerto Rico, honors Luis Muñoz-Rivera, Puerto Rican patriot, journalist, and poet, born this date in 1859.

18 **Nelson Mandela**, leader in the fight against apartheid in South Africa, was born in 1918.

19 **Edgar Degas**, French painter noted for his paintings of ballet dancers, was born in 1834. • The **first women's rights convention** in America was held in Seneca Falls, New York, in 1848.

20 **Moon Day** is the anniversary of the first landing on the moon in 1969 by astronauts Neil Armstrong, Edwin Aldrin, and Michael Collins. Armstrong was the first to walk on the moon's surface.

22 **Alexander Calder**, creator of magnificent mobiles, was born in 1898.

25 **Puerto Rico Constitution Day** commemorates the proclamation of Puerto Rico's Constitution in 1952.

26 **New York Ratification Day** (11th state, 1788).

28 **The first singing telegram** was sent in 1933, supposedly to singer Rudy Vallee on his 32nd birthday.

30 **Emily Brontë**, best known for *Wuthering Heights*, was born in 1818. • Automobile pioneer **Henry Ford** was born in 1863.

Anti-Boredom Month If anyone is bored, challenge her or him with **reproducible** activity page 90. (Answers: 1, Amy; 2, Dan; 3, Jen; 4, Peter; 5, Andy.)

National Ice Cream Day Here's a quick and easy recipe for making your own ice cream. For each portion, you'll need a soup can and a container big enough to set the can inside, leaving an empty space of about 2" around it. Sprinkle

some salt into the bottom of a container and set the can on top. Cover the can with aluminum foil, and pack a layer of ice around it, sprinkling salt on top. Continue layering ice and salt until the can is at least half-submerged. Remove or break open the foil cover. Pour a half-cup milk, one tablespoon sugar, one tablespoon sweetened condensed milk, and one or two drops vanilla extract into the can. About every two or three minutes, use a spoon to scrape the frozen mixture from the side of the can into the center. The ice cream will be ready to eat in about fifteen minutes. Yum!

July 4 Happy birthday, U.S.A! Have a parade with rhythm instruments the children make themselves. Then have a **Fourth of July** picnic featuring a red, white, and blue dessert—vanilla ice cream with strawberries and blueberries.

July 9 Hold your own **quilting bee**. Give each child a quilting-square pattern to color in any way he or she chooses. Then tape their squares together to make a multi-colored patchwork bulletin-board display. See **reproducible** activity page 91.

July 14 On **Woody Guthrie's** birthday, teach the class Woody's best loved song, "This Land Is Your Land."

July 20 On **Moon Day**, make sure everyone understands that the moon doesn't shine by itself. It reflects the light from the sun. To show how this is possible, darken the room, and hold up a mirror. Ask one of the students to shine a flashlight on the mirror. The light that seems to be shining out of the mirror is really from the flashlight.

July 22 Make all kinds of mobiles, a la **Calder**.

July 28 Make up **singing telegrams** to send to other classes. (Better check with other teachers, first.)

Name _____   Date _____

Who's Who

What are these children's names? You can tell by what's in their lockers. Write the correct name under each face.

| _____ | _____ | _____ | _____ | _____ |
| **LOCKER 1** | **LOCKER 2** | **LOCKER 3** | **LOCKER 4** | **LOCKER 5** |

Use these clues...

1. Amy and Jen have the same jacket.
2. Dan and Amy both play in the school band.
3. Andy plays on a different team from Peter and Jen.

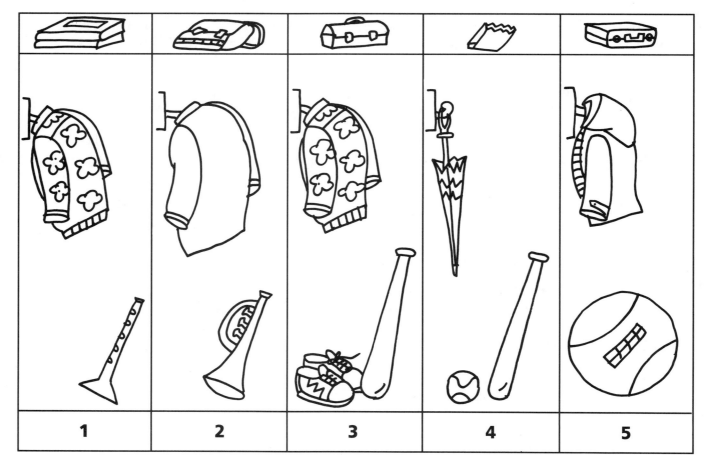

Do Your Part

Color the quilting square. Use any colors you choose. Then cut out your square.
Your work will become part of a beautiful class quilt.

AUGUST

Old Dog lay in the summer sun
Much too lazy to rise and run.

—from "Sunning,"
by James S. Tippet

August Is . . .

National Eye Exam Month   National Water Quality Month

Special Weeks in August

International Clown Week (first full week)
National Smile Week (first full week)
National Aviation Week (third full week)

Special Days in August

Friendship Day The first Sunday in August celebrates friendship.
Family Day The second Sunday in August is for families to enjoy together.

August Events

1 **Francis Scott Key**, who wrote the words to "The Star Spangled Banner," was born in 1779. • **Colorado Admission Day** (38th state, 1876).

2 On this day in 1776, about 50 of the 56 signers affixed their names, making this the official anniversary of the **Signing of the Declaration of Independence**.

5 **Neil Armstrong**, astronaut and first person to walk on the moon, was born in 1930.

6 **Alexander Fleming**, who won the Nobel Prize for his discovery of penicillin, was born in 1881. • **Lucille Ball** was born in 1911. Happy birthday to Lucy, leading lady of TV comedy for three decades!

7 **Ralph Bunche**, statesman and winner of the Nobel Peace Prize, was born in 1904.

8 **Sara Teasdale**, noted for her lovely nature poems, was born in 1884.

10 **Missouri Admission Day** (24th state, 1821).

11 In Van Buren, Iowa, "popcorn capital of the world," it's time for the **Popcorn Festival**.

12 **Cecil B. DeMille**, pioneer filmmaker best known for cinematic spectacles featuring casts of thousands (*The Ten Commandments*, *The Greatest Show on Earth*), was born in 1881.

13 **Lucy Stone**, eloquent advocate of women's rights and the abolition of slavery, was born in 1818. • **Annie Oakley** was born in 1860. She is legendary for her marksmanship, and was a star of Buffalo Bill's Wild West Show for many years. • Famed movie director **Alfred Hitchcock** was born in 1899.

14 **Middle Children's Day** salutes children born in the middle of the family. Missing out on the privileges of both big sisters and baby brothers, they deserve a special day of their own. • **Julia Child**, cooking authority and TV personality, was born in 1912.

15 **Edna Ferber**, novelist and playwright, was born in 1887.

17 **David Crockett**, better known as "Davy," famed frontiersman and adventurer, was born in 1786.

18 **Virginia Dare**, born on this date in 1587, was the first child born of English parents in the New World. • **The Nineteenth Amendment** to the U.S. Constitution, which gave the right to vote to women, was ratified in 1920.

19 **National Aviation Day** is celebrated on this date, the birth date of **Orville Wright**, born in 1871. • **Ogden Nash**, the writer of some of the funniest poems in the English language, was born in 1902. • **Gene Roddenberry**, creator of the TV series, "Star Trek," was born in 1921.

21 **Hawaii Admission Day** (50th state, 1959).

22 **Claude Debussy**, French composer, was born in 1862.

25 **Kiss-and-Make-Up Day** is the day to let bygones be bygones.

26 **Women's Equality Day** has been celebrated on this date since 1973.

27 The **first play** to be presented in the North American colonies, *Ye Bare and Ye Cubb*, by Phillip Alexander Bruce, was performed in Accomac, Virginia, in 1655. Three local residents were arrested and fined for acting in the play.

30 **Mary Shelley**, author of the novel *Frankenstein*, was born in 1797.

August Activities

National Water Quality Month Show the students one kind of test for water quality, and introduce an important chemistry concept at the same time. From a store that sells aquarium supplies, buy an inexpensive pH test kit. Follow the directions to test your local water for acidity. If you can get a sample of water from another location, it might be interesting to compare.

International Clown Week Have a clown show. Make costumes. Use special wash-off paint to decorate children's faces.

Friendship Day Joyce C. Hall, the man who founded Hallmark Cards, had the idea for Friendship Day. In 1935, Congress made it official. Provide all kinds of materials for children to make their own friendship cards to give or send to their pals. Use the instructions and pattern on **reproducible** pages 95 and 96 to make pop-up friendship cards. Have the children write their own messages inside.

August 8 On **Sara Teasdale's** birthday, read one of her poems to the class. Since August is a big month for shooting stars, they will enjoy this one.

The Falling Star
I saw a star slide down the sky,
Blinding the north as it went by,
Too burning and too quick to hold,
Too lovely to be bought or sold,
Good only to make wishes on
And then forever to be gone.

August 30 Mary Shelley was married to the poet, Percy Bysshe Shelley. Mary and her husband once spent a summer vacation in Switzerland with another famous English poet, Lord Byron. Every night, they told each other ghost stories.

Byron liked Mary's story about the "mad scientist" Frankenstein so much, he suggested she write it down. Invite your class to have a ghost-story session. Let one student start with, "It was a dark and stormy night, when..." Then have the other children take turns picking up the spooky story in mid-sentence until the end. Who knows? Maybe a new classic will be born on this day.

Friendship Pop-Up

Use these instructions and patterns to make friendship pop-up cards. Write your own message on your card.

Butterfly Pop-Up Card

1. Cut out the outlined rectangle.

2. Fold it in half on the center dotted line.

3. Cut on the solid lines.

4. Open the center fold.

5. Fold down on the *outside* dotted lines.

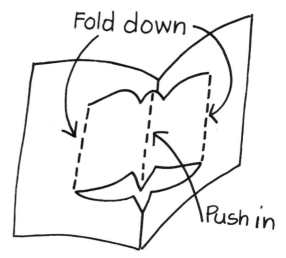
Fold down
Push in

Have a Happy Day!

6. Push the center dotted line *into* the card, and fold it.

7. Open up the card, cut another sheet of paper the same size, and fold it in half. The side of the card with the lines on it is the *outside*. Tape the plain folded paper to the outside of your card so the lines won't show. Now fold the whole card closed.

8. Open the card. The butterfly shape will pop up! Draw a smiling face on the butterfly. Cut out antennae and paste them on the butterfly's head.

9. Write a message that begins on the outside of the card and ends on the inside.

Butterfly Pop-Up Pattern

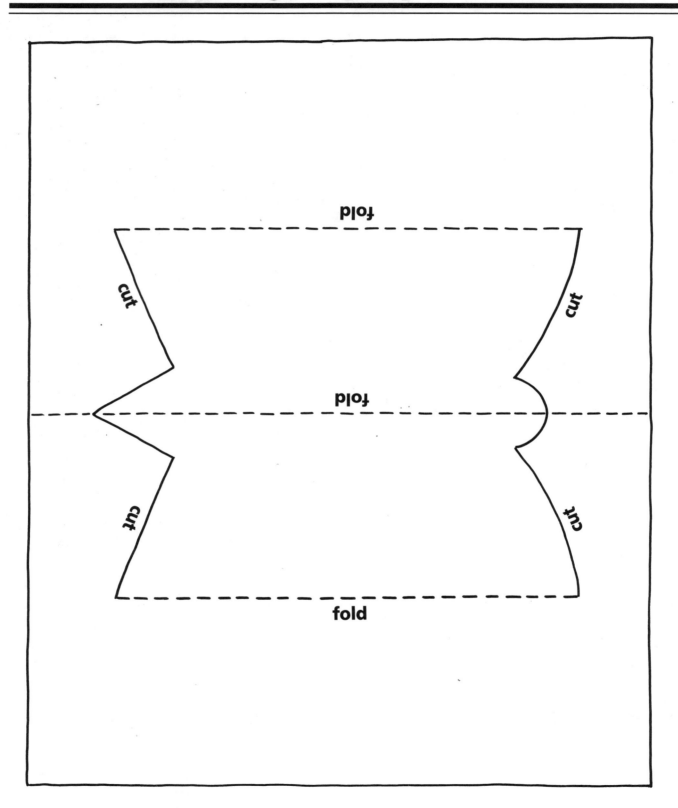